Cornerstones of Freedom

The Story of
THE
NEW ENGLAND
WHALERS

By R. Conrad Stein

Illustrated by Tom Dunnington

CHILDRENS PRESS, CHICAGO

Library of Congress Cataloging in Publication Data

Stein, R. Conrad.
The story of the New England whalers.

(Cornerstones of freedom)
Summary: The history of whaling in New
England from the early eighteenth century to
its decline when oil was discovered in the
mid-nineteenth century.
1. Whaling—Juvenile literature. 2. Whale-
men—New England—Juvenile literature.
[1. Whaling—New England. 2. New England
—Economic conditions] I. Dunnington, Tom, ill.
II. Title. III. Series.
SH381.S795   639'.28   81-18107
ISBN 0-516-04634-9   AACR2

It was a calm morning in 1845 as the whaling ship *Emigrant* cruised in the South Atlantic. The ship had twenty-one crew members. One of them was sixteen-year-old Ben E. S. Ely. He had signed on the whale ship seeking adventure. So far he had found only boredom. "A whaleman's life is one of either dull monotony, or of thrilling excitement, " Ely later wrote.

On the mast high above Ely's ship stood a lookout. He scanned the waves looking for spouts of water. Whales are mammals and have to breathe air. When they exhale they blow a spout of water high above them. Suddenly the lookout saw a telltale geyser of water. It came from the back of a huge whale.

"There she blows! " shouted the lookout.

The words struck like lightning on the deck of the *Emigrant.* The crew lowered the small whaleboats. Like spiders, the men scurried down ropes and climbed into the boats. Young Ely trembled with excitement. This was the first whale he had ever hunted. Finally he would experience the adventure he had dreamed about.

Three of the *Emigrant's* whaleboats rowed after the whale. Each boat held six crewmen and one officer. While rowing, the officer shouted to the men to pull the oars harder. As Ben Ely wrote, "At first they will beg you to pull, and then curse you. 'Oh! Do pull my dear fellows. Do pull...pull you lubbers! Pull or I will heave this lance through your heart!' "

The crew rowed while the whale's back bobbed in and out of the water in front of them. The officer knew just how to approach the whale—from behind so the animal would not sense the danger.

"Steady, lads. Steady," the officer said to the oarsmen. "Now lift your oars. Harpooner on your feet. Stand by your iron."

In the front of the boat, the harpooner stood holding the harpoon over his head like a snake about to strike. He waited until the whaleboat's bow practically crashed into the whale's back. Then he hurled his harpoon. The barbed end buried itself deep in the whale's back. For a second the ocean seemed as silent as a graveyard.

"Stern all," yelled the officer. "Row for your lives!"

Furiously, Ely and his shipmates paddled backward. When the whale felt the pain of the harpoon,

he might jump his full length out of the water. Any boat nearby would be dashed to bits.

The whale burst out of the water with an ear-splitting roar. "The roar of a right whale, when wounded, is terrific," wrote Ely. "I have heard it at a distance of four miles." With a splash that sounded like a thunderclap, the whale disappeared beneath the sea.

The men on Ely's boat waited. What would the whale do? It might dive. Two thousand feet of rope were coiled on the deck of the whaleboat. One end was tied to the harpoon. If the whale decided to dive, the crew would hold the rope taut and hope the whale would not play out their entire line.

This whale decided to dash over the surface of the water. Dragging the small boat behind him, the mighty whale took Ely and his shipmates on what was like a wild roller-coaster ride. At the dizzying speed of twenty miles per hour, the whale hauled the boat through the waves. Often the boat was pulled so swiftly that it skipped over the water like a flat stone thrown onto a pond. Whalemen called this madcap dash a "Nantucket sleigh ride."

Finally the whale tired himself out and floated quietly. This was the moment the crew had been waiting for, and they rowed closer for the kill. The officer grabbed an eleven-foot-long spear called a lance. Taking careful aim, the officer threw the

lance at a spot on the whale's back above his windpipe. When the lance struck, "the whale roared and snapped with its immense jaws," wrote Ely, "and in his fury lashed the blue seas around him into a bloody foam."

After a few minutes of wild thrashing about, the whale floated lifeless in the water. Blood gushed from his wounds. A flock of sea birds hovered near his body. Their beaks dipped into the water as they drank the blood. The flutter of birds' wings seemed to sound taps for this giant of the sea.

Ely and his shipmates breathed a sigh of relief. Their dangerous hunt was over. But the kill meant the beginning of hours of backbreaking work.

First the huge whale had to be hauled to the ship and tied alongside. Then came the difficult tasks called *cutting in* and *trying out*. Cutting in meant peeling off the whale's blubber. Trying out meant cooking that blubber into oil.

In the 1700s and 1800s, whales were hunted for their oil. All over the world people used lamps that burned whale oil. Those lamps were the brightest source of light the people had. There were also some uses for a bonelike substance from the whale's mouth called baleen. Baleen was often used to make stays for ladies' corsets. But men made fortunes in the trading of whale oil. It was sometimes called "liquid gold."

Once the whale was tied up alongside, the ship became a busy floating factory.

Cutting in was an immense butcher's job. Using knives with ten-foot-long handles, the men cut slits into the whale's skin. Then they hooked the skin to winches and peeled it off the whale's body. Underneath that skin lay about one foot of the yellow fat called blubber that produces the precious oil.

While the men were cutting in, schools of hungry sharks swam about the whale's body. The crew of the *Emigrant* tried to chase the sharks away by

stabbing at them with harpoons. The blubber covered the deck with a slick film of oil. One wrong move and a man could slip, fall into the sea, and become a meal for a shark.

The blubber was hauled to the deck in slabs that looked like gigantic blankets. It was then cut into smaller chunks for trying out.

In the middle of the deck stood a brick stove holding two brass kettles about the size of washtubs. This was called the *tryworks*. The stove burned either wood or whale oil. A crewman threw the

chunks of blubber into the hot trying kettles where they crackled and sizzled. Oil cooked out of the blubber the same way grease cooks out of bacon in a frying pan.

Around the clock the crew cut up the blubber and cooked it in the trying kettles. At night the blaze under the kettles made the ship look as if it were on fire. Rendering a huge whale into oil was a messy, smelly task. Sailors on merchant ships claimed they could smell a whaler long before they could see one.

It usually took forty-eight hours of furious work to process the whale's blubber into oil. The oil was put into barrels and stored in the hold of the ship. Then the men of the *Emigrant* once more began the search for whales. For Ben Ely the cycle of danger, followed by exhausting work, followed by weeks of boredom would continue. This was the life of a whaleman during the golden age of whaling.

Ely and his shipmates worked an ancient trade. Whaling in America was practiced long before the coming of Europeans.

An Englishman exploring the coast of Maine wrote about Indians hunting whales from canoes back in the year 1620. "With their arrows they shoot (the whale) to death; when they have killed him and dragged him to shore, they will call all their chief lords together and sing a song of joy...."

The whales hunted by the Indians had to be very small ones. No whale of ordinary size could be killed by arrows and hauled to shore with canoes.

European settlers in the New World quickly took up whaling. The most important whaling centers grew in New England ports. Whaling remained a New England industry for more than two hundred years.

In the early 1700s the country's leading whaling center developed on Nantucket Island. Nantucket is a rocky island about thirty miles off the coast of Massachusetts. Farming was difficult there. But Nantucket settlers could stand on their front porches and see whales spouting and playing in the waves. Naturally, Nantucketers turned to the sea for their living.

At first Nantucket whalemen hunted a type of whale called the *right whale*. Right whales usually swam near the coast. They were large and fought

hard when harpooned. But another type of whale was even larger, and fought like a demon. Bigger than the biggest dinosaurs that ever walked the earth, it could weigh eighty tons or more. This was the *sperm whale*. Its discovery changed whaling forever.

In 1712 a whaling ship commanded by Christopher Hussey sailed from Nantucket. The ship was soon caught up in a mighty storm. Howling winds and huge seas drove the little ship farther out in the Atlantic than any other New England whaler had ever been before. When the storm finally cleared, the crew of Hussey's ship could scarcely believe their eyes. All around them they saw the black shapes of whales. But these were not the familiar right whales. These whales were truly giants.

With skill and a lot of luck, Hussey's men managed to kill one of them. The animal put up a terrific fight. Hussey tied the whale alongside his ship and headed home. In those early days of whaling, the whales were processed into oil on shore instead of aboard the whaling ships.

At Nantucket, everyone turned out to look at the monster whale. When the sperm whale was processed, Nantucketers discovered that it rendered much more oil than did a right whale. Its oil was of better quality, too. And the whalemen later found out that the head of a sperm whale contained an oil that could be made into a superb candle wax.

Soon other ships went to sea to hunt the newly discovered sperm whale. Captains quickly learned that these whales liked deep water. The captains had not spotted sperm whales before because their ships had always hugged the coast. But to pursue whales in the deep water, whalemen needed larger ships with stoves and tryworks aboard. New and

better ships were built. They carried whalemen on long, heroic voyages.

Sailing the new ships, Nantucketers found herds of sperm whales at places they called *whale grounds*. Whale grounds were discovered near the island of Bermuda, across the ocean at the Azores, and in the Gulf of Mexico.

The taking of sperm whales meant prosperity for the New England whaling industry. By 1770, Nantucket claimed a fleet of 125 whaling ships. Whaling supported the island's entire population of 4,500. Also, a new whaling center was growing at New Bedford, Massachusetts.

NORTH AMERICA

New England

RIGHT WHALE

SPERM WHALE

SOUTH AMERICA

EMILIA

Cape Horn

But success worked against the New England whaling industry. As soon as new whale grounds were discovered, the whales there were quickly killed off.

Then, in 1788, a whaler called the *Emilia* attempted what was thought to be impossible. Seeking new whale grounds, the captain pointed his ship south and decided to round Cape Horn at the tip of South America. The captain wanted to try his luck in the Pacific Ocean. At Cape Horn, winds roared at a hundred miles an hour and waves towered fifty feet into the sky. The cape had been a graveyard for merchant ships twice the size of a whaler. No tiny whaling ship had ever dared to "round the Horn" before.

For twenty-one days the *Emilia* was caught in a gale that tossed her about like a toy boat in a bathtub. But when the ship finally emerged in the South Pacific, the crew discovered a whaleman's paradise. "I never saw so many large sperm whales all the time I have been in the business as I have this voyage," wrote Captain Shields of the *Emilia*.

After the *Emilia's* voyage, the New England coast buzzed with the news that the Pacific Ocean teemed with whales.

Now the great whale hunt was on in the far Pacific. Whalemen sailed out of New England on voyages that would last three, four, and even five years. The longest whaling voyage on record lasted an incredible eleven years. The pursuit of whales in the Pacific took New England men to exotic sunny islands. They saw strange birds and beasts. They met smiling girls with flowers in their hair. They also met fierce tribes of people who ate human flesh.

Whaleships ventured into both the Antarctic and Arctic oceans. Captains risked wrecking their ships while whipping around Cape Horn. Then they navigated through waters where Western men had never sailed before. And these risks were taken even before the men began their most dangerous job—the hunting of the mighty sperm whale.

In the early 1800s, New England whaling became more than just an industry. It became a great American adventure.

From all over the country men flocked to New England to hunt whales. There was little job discrimination in the whaling industry. Blacks and American Indians served on whaling ships alongside whites. They rose through the ranks to become harpooners, officers, and captains.

The pay on whaling ships was low. A crewman was paid a share of the profits of the voyage. An officer received a greater share than a deckhand. If the vessel's catch was poor, everyone's share was reduced. A harpooner named Nelson Haley earned $400 for a three-year voyage. Then the captain deducted the value of the clothes Haley had bought from the ship's store and advance pay he had drawn while on shore leave. When he left the ship, Haley's pay came to only $200. Haley later wrote that whaling was "a rather slow way to get rich."

Largely because of the low wages, whaling crews were made up of young men who were desperate for work. Usually only the officers were over thirty. Most of the deck crew were teenagers. And every whaleship employed one or two cabin boys. They could be as young as ten or twelve.

The crews who signed on whaling ships knew the job was dangerous. At a seaman's chapel in New Bedford, the men could read placards dedicated to some of the many whalemen who shipped out and never returned. The placards hang on the walls of that famous chapel today. They read: "In the memory of Quincy A. Harlow. . . aged 19 years, who fell overboard December 8, 1848, and was lost." "To the memory of John W. Samson. . . who died of consumption at sea April 8, 1848, aged 18 years." "In the memory of Wm. Swain. . . this worthy man, after fastening to a whale, was carried overboard by the line, and drowned May 19, 1848."

Many young men ignored the dangers and low wages and signed on whaling ships because they wanted travel and adventure. Whaling usually gave them plenty of excitement. But the new whalemen were always dismayed by the awful boredom of endless sailing in search of whales.

To combat the boredom, whalemen often turned to scrimshaw. Scrimshaw was the practice of carving whale teeth into useful and beautiful things. Using jackknives, whalemen made whistles, cane handles, candlesticks, figures of birds and animals, and clothespins out of ivory whale teeth. Some scrimshaw pieces are now displayed in museums where they are hailed as objects of art. But to the whaleman, scrimshaw was simply making good use of two things he had plenty of—whale teeth and time.

Gams were another relief from boredom. A gam took place when two or more whaleships met at sea and tied up together so the crews could exchange visits. A gam could go on for as long as a week.

When there were no whales in sight, whaling was an unhurried life.

The men who signed on whaleships for excitement and danger soon found it. Shipwrecks were common among whalers. A shipwreck in the South Seas could strand a whole crew on a strange island with hostile natives.

A whaler called the *Oeno* was wrecked on a coral reef in the Fiji Islands in 1825. The natives murdered all of the twenty-man crew save one. The island chief spared the life of a man from Nantucket named William Cary. Cary lived with the Fiji Islanders for the next two years, entirely cut off from his own people. He learned the native language and even traveled with the tribe on war parties. While walking on the beach one day, Cary was astonished to discover another white man. The other man's name was David Whippey. He had deserted from a whaling ship nine years earlier, and had been living on a neighboring island. The people on that island had even made Whippey their chief. When the two men talked they discovered they were both from Nantucket, and had been friends and playmates when they were children on the other side of the world.

Cary, the shipwrecked whaleman, eventually got back to New England. He later wrote a book about his years with the Fiji Island natives. Whippey, the deserter, lived for the rest of his life on the Fiji Islands. He enjoyed being a chief.

A famous and dreadful shipwreck occurred in 1820. The *Essex* was hunting whales in the Pacific near the Equator when the crew was suddenly horrified to see a huge whale plunging out of the ocean right toward their ship. "He came down on us with full speed and struck the ship with his head," wrote an officer. "The ship brought up as suddenly and violently as if she had struck a rock." The *Essex* sank, leaving the men drifting in whaleboats. This was perhaps the only time on record that a whale succeeded in destroying an entire whaleship.

The survivors of the *Essex* sailed their whaleboats toward the coast of South America—more than one thousand miles away. Rain squalls kept the men supplied with water, but their food ran out. One by one the men died of hunger. Finally, the desperate survivors turned to cannibalism. They ate the flesh of one of their dead. And in one boat the men drew lots to choose a victim. That man was killed to provide flesh for the others. Of the twenty-man crew of the

Essex only eight survived their ordeal at sea. Years later, the captain tried to write about the man who had been killed. The captain wrote a few words but then had to stop. He said, "I can tell no more—my head is on fire at the recollection."

The greatest adventures the whalemen experienced were battles with the powerful beasts they hunted. Stories of whales and the fights they put up were told from crew to crew. Those stories became legends.

One legendary whale had a white hump and was called New Zealand Tom. He was famous because it seemed impossible to kill him. In dozens of battles whalemen harpooned him only to see him break away. A whaleship named *Adonis* finally took New Zealand Tom. When his body was hauled to the ship, the crew found a dozen harpoons rusting in his hide.

A mighty whale named Timor Jack enjoyed attacking whaleboats. He either crushed the boats with his jaws or capsized them with a switch of his tail. Timor Jack's aggressiveness led to his death.

Because they knew he liked to attack moving objects, one crew tied a barrel to the stern of their ship. Timor Jack chased the bouncing barrel just the way a trout would chase a lure. The crew hauled the barrel close to the ship and were able to land two harpoons in the back of the huge whale.

Easily the most famous whale the New Englanders ever faced was Mocha Dick. One whaleman said his hide was "white as wool." He was first sighted near the Mocha Islands off Chile in 1810. For the next thirty years Mocha Dick reversed the roles between whales and whalemen. Mocha Dick became the hunter while the whalemen became the hunted.

Mocha Dick seemed to have a curious intelligence and an almost human hatred for whalemen. He once acted as a guard to a harpooned whale so that the whale could escape. Another time he played dead to lure some whaleboats close to him. He then attacked, crushing the whaleboats and killing several men. Mocha Dick fought at least one hundred furious battles with whalemen. Always the huge animal escaped. In his wake he left dozens of smashed whaleboats and thirty dead whalemen.

It is no wonder that Mocha Dick became the subject of the most famous of all whaling books. In the early 1840s, a struggling writer named Herman Melville signed on a whaling ship. He deserted in the South Seas, lived for a while with the natives, and finally worked his way back to New England on a navy ship. In 1851, Melville published his classic novel *Moby Dick*. The story tells of a mad captain whose only purpose in life was to kill a white whale called Moby Dick. Because of his madness, the captain allowed the whale to destroy him, his ship, and his crew. The book became one of the greatest novels ever written by an American. *Moby Dick* explored the feelings one man held toward a whale. Other whalemen also wrote about their feelings toward whales. Almost nowhere in the writings of whalemen can one find words of sympathy for the whale. Instead, the whalemen's favorite saying was, "A dead whale or a stove boat." The word "stove" meant crushed or destroyed. They feared that if they did not kill the whale the whale would destroy their boat. The whalemen of old believed that whaling was a matter of kill or be killed.

Whales are still being killed today. Whale flesh is valuable as pet food and the oil is used in the chemical industry. But now whales are tracked with sonar, pursued in helicopters, and killed by guns that fire explosive shells. Because of these methods, whales are disappearing from the oceans.

Certainly the modern whaling industry kills more whales than did the New England whalers. In 1975 whalers killed 17,000 sperm whales. This was more than four times the number of sperm whales killed in 1846, the peak year for the old New England whaling industry. Limits on how many whales can be killed each year are set by the International Whaling Commission. In 1980 that agency allowed some 20,000 whales to be killed. But many scientists say that number is far too high. The scientists claim that whale fishing must be banned entirely for a period of at least ten years. If it is not, whales will disappear from the oceans forever.

The New England whaling industry reached its golden age during the 1830s, '40s, and '50s. During that time more than seven hundred American whaling ships plied the oceans. Brave Yankee whalemen carried their country's flag to every corner of the globe. They discovered new islands and charted new waterways. In the 1840s, an American navy lieutenant wrote: "Our whaling fleet may be said at this very date to whiten the Pacific Ocean with its canvas."

The end of New England whaling came not at sea, but in the state of Pennsylvania. In 1859 a man named Edwin Drake drilled an oil well in a Pennsylvania forest. The oil he struck burned brighter in lamps than whale oil did. Also, it was much less expensive than whale oil was.

American whaling continued even after the new oil came into use, but gradually whalemen sought other work and whaleships were junked. By 1906, only forty-two American whaleships sailed the seas. One of those was the *Charles W. Morgan*. That remarkable vessel served for eighty years as a whaleship. The *Charles W. Morgan* now rests at Mystic Seaport, Connecticut, where she is part of a museum complex. Today tourists climb aboard her to look at the brick tryworks and the cramped quarters where the men slept. The *Morgan* is the only American whaler left anywhere.

In ships like the *Morgan* many boys grew into manhood. Ben E. S. Ely, who chased his first whale at age sixteen, wrote: "To young men who long for hardships. . . I would say 'go to sea' and perhaps I should say to a father, who can do nothing else with a worthless refractory son, 'send him on a whaling voyage.' "

Ely also wrote about a religious experience he had while on board his whaling ship. Such experiences were common. Whalemen sailed small ships on immense oceans, and they battled the largest animals on the planet. It is no wonder their thoughts turned to a higher power. The Bible was their most popular book. And one of their favorite passages was from Psalms 107:

Others there are who go down to the sea in ships
and make their living on the wide waters.
These men have seen the acts of the Lord
and His marvelous doings in the deep.

About the Author

R. Conrad Stein was born and grew up in Chicago. He enlisted in the Marine Corps at the age of eighteen and served for three years. He then attended the University of Illinois where he received a bachelor's degree in history. He later studied in Mexico, earning an advanced degree from the University of Guanajuato. Mr. Stein is the author of many other books, articles, and short stories written for young people.

To finance his education, Mr. Stein worked as a merchant seaman. He has always had an interest in ships and life at sea. While researching this book, Mr. Stein traveled to Mystic Seaport, Connecticut, and New Bedford, Massachusetts, to study whaling lore firsthand.

Mr. Stein now lives in Pennsylvania with his wife, Deborah Kent, who is also a writer of books for young readers.

About the Artist

Tom Dunnington divides his time between book illustration and wildlife painting. He has done many books for Childrens Press, as well as working on textbooks, and is a regular contributor to "Highlights for Children." Tom lives in Oak Park, Illinois.